How Kids Play
Around the World

ALBATROS

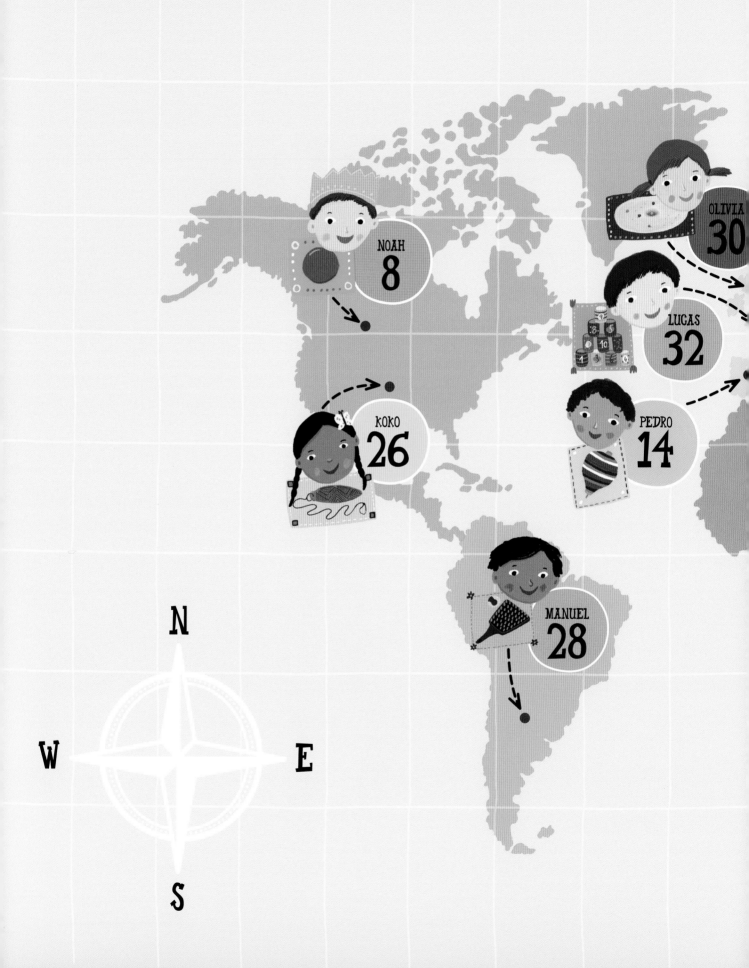

Fun and play go hand in hand with childhood

How many kids do you know who don't like to play? None, right? I would venture to say that enjoying playing—with toys, as well as games with friends—comes naturally to all kids. This can be said of ancient times, the recent past, and the present day. Archeological excavation and historical sources have proven beyond a doubt that people have played since the dawn of time. Quite simply, playing is in our blood.

Hooray! I'm the winner!

I can crawl just like a crab!

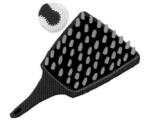

I'll be the one who jumps there first!

Learning through play

You may be surprised to learn that play is more than just fun: it is also extremely important. Indeed, it has been proven that playing is essential to a kid's development. Play teaches us about ourselves and the world around us. Games help us solve all kinds of problems that will crop up in our lives. So, carry on playing! You will be learning without realizing it. That's right—when you are being silly and enjoying yourself, you are actually developing. Great, isn't it?

Playing is fun!

Games from all over the world

Kids all over the world have their games. Some games and activities—such as skipping rope, shooting marbles, and spinning wooden tops—occur practically everywhere. Others are common only in some areas. In places where an ability to hunt was really important, for instance, it makes sense that kid's games focused on improving fitness, accuracy, and attention, thus making good hunters of them. Elsewhere, games were connected with religious ritual, tradition, and the beliefs and mythology of our ancestors. The world of child's play is incredibly diverse. Join us—won't you?—as we scoot around the world to take a look at it.

Can you catch me?

Look what I can do!

I'm looking for chocolate!

African Games

HI! MY NAME'S **ZHENGA**, AND I COME FROM SUNNY **AFRICA**, A CONTINENT OF GREAT NATURAL BEAUTY AND MANY MAGNIFICENT ANIMALS. I LOVE ANIMALS. WHEN I GROW UP, I WOULD LIKE TO TAKE CARE OF THEM. LIKE EVERY CHILD, I ENJOY PLAYING WITH MY FRIENDS. OUR TRADITIONAL GAMES ARE GREAT. COME ALONG AND SEE FOR YOURSELF.

1 Ampe

One of my favorite games is Ampe. Two kids, one of them the leader, face each other. As they jump up together, they clap and thrust one foot forward. If the leader and their opponent have the same foot forward, the leader wins the point. If the feet are different, the opponent becomes the leader.

2 Spectators of Ampe

The ancient entertainment of Ampe originated in the West African country of Ghana. In the distant past, it was played mainly by adults. Spectators from neighboring villages would gather to watch Ampe tournaments lasting several days. Successful competitors were regarded as stars in their locales.

3 Kutoda

A game called Kudoda, from Zimbabwe, demands speed, quick reflexes, and deft fingers. A group of friends sit around a bowl filled with marbles (or pebbles). The first player takes a marble and tosses it into the air. Before it drops, they try to collect as many marbles as they can, using only one hand.

10 Skipping rope has a long history

From drawings found in tombs from Ancient Egypt, we know that skipping rope has been popular entertainment for many centuries. At first, only men enjoyed this pastime, but women and girls soon joined in.

4 Nyama, Nyama

One of my favorite games is Nyama, from Kenya. It needs at least three players. The player appointed as the leader shouts the name of an animal. If this animal is a carnivore, the other players jump up. If it's a herbivore, the players stay grounded. They soon may become so confused that they wrongly jump up to greet the herbivorous antelope.

9 Tinko tinko

Tinko Tinko is a great Nigerian game that requires a partner, not an opponent. The players sing "Tinko Tinko" as they clap and touch palms. As the game goes on, the clapping and palm-touching speeds up. The game ends when one of the players mixes up the actions.

8 Skipping rope

Skipping rope is one of our favorite games, even though it makes us sweat. The best skipping is when two friends face each other, each turning one end of the rope as they wait for the right moment to jump over it. Sometimes we compete— the winner is the one who makes the most jumps.

HELLO, I AM
ZHENGA

7 Military exercises

Tug of War was popular in Ancient Egypt, Cambodia, India, Greece, and China too. I even heard about a Chinese emperor who used this game to train his soldiers.

6 Tug of War

Tug of War, another of our traditional games, strengthens the muscles. Two teams, each with a leader, tug on opposite ends of a rope. The team that succeeds in pulling the opponent toward them is named the winner.

5 Soccer—what a game!

Everyone, boys and girls alike, loves playing soccer. Tell me something I don't know, you say. We make our own soccer balls, using fabrics, old stockings, string, and various packing materials. A ball like this is more fun than one from the store, believe me.

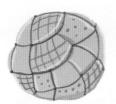

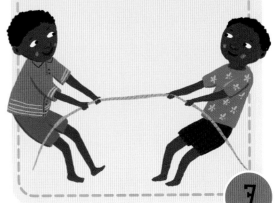

North American Games

HI! MY NAME'S **NOAH**. I WAS BORN HERE IN THE **USA**, JUST LIKE MY PARENTS, GRANDPARENTS, AND EVEN GREAT-GRANDPARENTS. ALTHOUGH I LIVE IN THE MODERN WORLD, TO TELL THE TRUTH I'M HAPPIEST WHEN MY FRIENDS AND I PUT DOWN OUR CELLPHONES, FORGET ABOUT COMPUTERS, AND THROW OURSELVES INTO OUTDOOR GAMES. THERE'S NOTHING BETTER THAN REAL-WORLD FUN!

10 Marco Polo

Many of our games take place in swimming pools. Marco Polo, named after the famous medieval explorer, is a fun water game. One player closes their eyes and calls out, "Marco The others all reply, "Polo," and try to stay ou of the way as the caller swims towards their voices to catch one of them.

HEY, I'M
NOAH

1 King of the Hill

I *never* get tired of this game. Want to try it? Just find an elevated place, like a hill or a pile, and stand on it, along with three other players. A fourth will try to push you from the hill and take your place up there. I'm unbeatable at this game—no one has ever pushed me from the hill. I'm the King of the Hill!

2 Hula-Hooping

Twirling a hoop around your waist is fun for girls and boys alike. The best at this game can twirl the hoop from waist to neck—unbelievable, right?! Hula-hooping came to us from Hawaii.

3 Dodgeball

Here in America, we love ball games. One of our favorites is dodgeball. The rules are simple. Two teams face each other. The players of one team throw small balls at the the other team. If a player is struck by a ball, they are knocked out. This game depends on speed, especially speedy reflexes. It is super fun!

9 The Floor is Lava

Quite simply, we pretend that the floor is made of lava, causing us to move from one point to the next without touching the ground. *Help, I'm falling!* When I fall, I'm out of the game.

8 Duck, Duck, Goose

This game is from our preschool years. Everyone sits in a circle while the picker walks around, tapping each of us on the shoulder and calling us "duck"—until finally they call one of us "goose." The goose now chases the picker around the circle, trying to reach the vacant space before the picker does.

7 Capture the Flag

I love this game! It is played by two teams divided into two territories. Each flag is planted in the opponent's territory, and each team must try to get their flag and return it to their own base without getting caught.

6 Sharks and Minnows

This is a classic pool chase. By its name, it should be clear who chases who. Pursued by the shark, the minnows try to get from one end of the pool to the other. The minnow who gets caught becomes the shark. Thanks to this game, I've learned to swim like a fish!

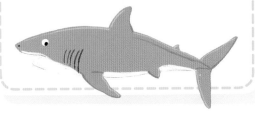

4 Hot Potato

This game also requires a ball. Players stand in a circle, sing a song, and toss a ball around. The player who receives the ball must pass it to another player as quickly as possible. Whoever is holding the ball when the song ends is out.

5 Handball

As I said, we Americans love ball games. Another one is called Handball. All you need for it is a ball, a wall, and a marked area (or court) into which the ball can land. You bounce the ball on the ground so that it rebounds onto the wall. When it bounces off the wall, the other player must strike it back against the wall using the flat of the hand. The ball can't leave the court.

New Zealand Games

HI! MY NAME'S **MAIA**, AND I LIVE IN **NEW ZEALAND**, AN ISLAND NATION IN THE PACIFIC OCEAN. THE ORIGINAL PEOPLE OF NEW ZEALAND ARE THE MĀORI. MANY OF OUR COUNTRY'S TRADITIONAL GAMES ARE MĀORI IN ORIGIN.

1 Tititorea

Tititorea is one of these traditional games. Two players kneel on the ground, with a short stick in each hand, which they pass to each other in trained movements in time to accompanying chants. Slow at first, the movements speed up until the players are throwing the sticks to each other.

2 Sharpness and quick reactions

Tititorea is hundreds of years old. It was originally about more than just having fun. The Māori used it to train their sharpness and quick reactions.

3 Poi

If you believe that twirling a ball connected to a string is a piece of cake, you will soon change your mind if you try Poi, another traditional Māori game. Can you twirl a ball clockwise with one hand and counterclockwise with the other? I can't—and that's just a beginner's trick! The real art is to master tracing complex geometric shapes.

10 Time for fun and games

Most Māori games were played during times of rest, when the harvest was over. Although games served to teach a variety of skills, people enjoyed them. And they still do today.

HELLO, I AM **MAIA**

4 Supple wrists

Poi helped Māori hunters develop shoulder strength and improve coordination. Māori women used this game to make their wrists more flexible.

9 Hipitoitoi

For this game, there are four positions: Both thumbs up. Both thumbs down. Left thumb up and right thumb down. Right thumb up and left thumb down. The defender flashes one of the hand positions and says, "Hipitoitoi," while the challenger flashes a different one. If they do the same position, the defender gets a point.

8 Ruru

If you get tired of twirling the poi, try another Māori game with it that, like Tititorea, is hundreds of years old. As you chant a Māori rhyme, you throw the poi into the air and catch it before it hits the ground. If you have to grab it by the string, the task is even harder! Each round starts where the poi was last caught.

7 Kite

The Māori game of Kite is really good fun. Two players are blindfold, and each holds a rattle known as a Ki Paua. The rattle makes a sound with every step the players take, indicating where they are. The winner is the first to find their opponent and touch them.

6 Poi Rākau

Poi Rākau is another game once played by Māori warriors for training purposes. Players form a circle, with the player known as the Commander at the center. Every player in the circle holds a long stick. After the Commander cries "Left!" the players in the circle release their stick, move one position to the left, and grab the stick released by the player to their left. Throughout, none of the sticks may touch the ground. It's hard work and requires intense concentration.

5 The power of the warrior

You have surely noticed that the aim of most of these traditional Māori games was to improve indigenous warriors' dexterity, speed of reaction or thought, and physical prowess.

Finnish Games

HI! MY NAME'S **JUHANI**, AND I'M A **FINN**. PEOPLE TALK OF FINLAND AS A LAND OF A THOUSAND LAKES; IN FACT, WE HAVE OVER 150,000 OF THEM. WE FINNS HAVE PLAYED AND COMPETED SINCE ANCIENT TIMES. BUT ENOUGH TALK: I'M OFF TO THE PLAYING FIELD. WANT TO JOIN ME?

1 Crab Ball Tag

The traditional game of Crab Ball Tag is popular with preschool kids, us older kids, and even grown-ups. We have a lot of fun with it! We assume the basic pose of a crab, with our weight resting on our hands and feet and our bellies pushed up. Only like this are we allowed to move.

2 The rules of Crab Ball Tag

Crab Ball Tag is played by at least five people. Only one of these is not a crab: the crab-hunter. The hunter's task is to catch a crab by hitting it with a rubber ball between the neck and the waist— as gently as possible, of course! A caught crab becomes the hunter, and the hunter becomes a crab.

HELLO, I AM **JUHANI**

3 How can a crab defend itself?

Crabs aren't helpless against the hunter's attacks. When the hunter chooses you as the target, you should try to kick or head-butt the ball away. We older kids improve the game by playing it with two balls and two hunters. Ouch! I got hit! I guess I wasn't paying attention.

9 Ketju

The game of Kejtu (meaning "chain") is hilarious! All players but one (the challenger) form a circle and weave themselves together in various ways while holding hands. Then the challenger tries to unweave them. It sounds simple, but a clever weave will give the challenger no chance, trust me.

8 How to play Mölkky?

To play Mölkky, we set up numbered pins in the shape of a triangle. We then try to knock these pins over with the throwing pin. If you knock over one pin, you score the number of points marked on that pin. If you knock over more than one, your score is the number of pins you have knocked over.

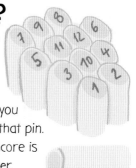

7 Mölkky

Further evidence of we Finns' fondness for skittles is found in Mölkky, another game featuring wooden pins. From the south of Finland, it harkens back to the distant times of the Vikings.

6 Gravel or ice?

Finnish skittles is best played on a flat surface covered with gravel. In winter, however, we play it on a snowy field or a frozen lake, sometimes finding time to build a snowman in the process.

4 Kyykkä

Kyykkä—also called Finnish skittles—is a centuries-old game once played in remote villages, involving wooden pins called skittles. It was rediscovered in the late 19th century by a Finnish writer and photographer.

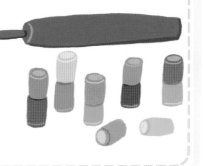

5 Away with the skittles!

The aim of Kyykkä is to clear the playing area of skittles as quickly as possible by throwing a rounded, wooden, handled bat at them. The more skittles the player hits, the more successful they are.

13

Spanish Games

HI! WE'RE **LOLA** AND **PEDRO**, A SISTER AND BROTHER FROM **SPAIN**. AS THERE'S NO SCHOOL TODAY, WE HAVE MET UP WITH OUR FRIENDS TO ENJOY OUR FREE TIME. COME ALONG WITH US AND FIND OUT HOW WE KIDS PLAY IN SPAIN.

1 Tripas de Gato

On a rainy day, when you don't feel much like doing anything, a game with a strange name—Cat's Guts!—is sure to improve your mood. To play it, you need paper, colored pencils, and at least one other player. A quick look at our results will show you how the game got its name.

2 How to play Cat's Guts

On your sheet of paper, draw ten pairs of objects: hearts, wheels, stars—whatever you want. Then try to join one of the pairs with a single unbroken stroke of a colored pencil. The other player will do the same using a pencil of a different color, without lifting it from the page or crossing the line you have drawn. And so it goes on until one of the players breaks or crosses a line, thereby losing the game.

9 Spinning trompo

This is a trompo, a traditional Spanish cone-shaped spinning top. Some players learn to work wonders with it. Although playing with it may look easy, it is anything but. I'll probably never tame my Spanish trompo!

HELLO, WE ARE **LOLA** AND **PEDRO**

3 Sea and Land

When we want a good workout, we play the game Mar y Tierra. Players divide the playing area into two halves—one representing the sea, the other the land—before placing themselves in the middle. One of the players calls to the sea. The rest of us jump to where the sea is. Then the first player calls to the land, causing us to jump to the other half of the playing area. The caller wants to confuse us so that we jump wrong.

1, 2, 3 Escondite Inglés

Players of this game laugh a lot too. One faces a wall, counting to three as the others try to reach the wall at top speed. When the counter shouts "Escondite Inglés!"—"English Hideout!"—the others must be still. If anyone moves, they must change places with the counter before the game can begin again.

7 Seek and you will find

There's another traditional Spanish game I've enjoyed playing since I was little. It's about finding hidden things. When there are two players, the first does the hiding and the second does the seeking. The seeker is helped by the words *frío* and *caliente*. The former tells him to look elsewhere; the latter tells him he is getting close.

6 Help! Run!

When the wolf cries "Estoy con hambre," we break from the circle and flee. The wolf chases us. The player caught by the wolf plays the wolf in the next round. It's so exciting because you never know when the wolf will cry that he's hungry. Sometimes he puts on practically every imaginable item of clothing before he does so.

4 Rock Paper Scissors

This game is popular all over the Spanish-speaking world. Two players face each other and chant, "Rock, Paper, Scissors." As the chant ends, they simultaneously form one of the three shapes with an outstretched hand. If the two symbols are the same, you start over. If one shows rock and the other paper, the paper wins. If one shows paper and the other scissors, the scissors win. If one shows rock and the other scissors, the rock wins.

5 Are You the Wolf?

This "wolf" game is really exciting. One player, the Wolf, stands beyond the rest of the players, who walk around in a circle. From time to time, the circle stops and its members call to the wolf, "Are you the wolf?" The wolf mostly answers by putting on an item of clothing. Occasionally, however, his response is to cry, "Estoy con hambre!"—"I'm hungry!"— and heaven forbid when he does.

German Games

HI! ALLOW ME TO INTRODUCE MYSELF. MY NAME'S **ULRICH**, WHICH NO DOUBT TELLS YOU THAT I COME FROM **GERMANY**. IT IS SAID THAT GERMANS HAVE A KEEN SENSE OF ORDER AND LIKE EVERYTHING JUST SO. WHEN WE PLAY, HOWEVER, WE GET TRULY CARRIED AWAY.

1 Topfschlagen

Germany is famous for its high-quality chocolate. And one of my favorite games is all about it. You hide a pot filled with chocolate somewhere in the room. Then you blindfold the players and give them a stick or a wooden spoon, which they use to search for the choco-treasure. After the chocolate is found, it is eaten, of course.

2 Schokoladenessen

My second favorite game is about chocolate too. My friends and I sit around a table with a chocolate bar in the middle. Each of us is given a knife and fork and various items of clothing, including a pair of mittens. The players roll a die. The first to throw a six must put on the clothes and begin to eat the chocolate using the knife and fork. Meanwhile, the other players continue to try to throw a six, so that they can take over from the first in the chocolate-eating.

9 Another first

Margarete Steiff's first teddy bear was and looked homemade. Later, in 1902, Margarete's nephew Richard Steiff made a teddy bear with moving limbs. Before long, this new toy was hugely popular all over the world.

HELLO, I AM **ULRICH**

3 German chocolate

In Germany, the making of high-quality, great-tasting chocolate has a long tradition: the very first German chocolate-making factory opened at the end of the 18th century. So it's no surprise that this sweet product is represented in our traditional games.

8 Teddy bear

I can't imagine my bedroom without a teddy bear in it. It was the first toy made for both girls and boys. Before the teddy arrived, all toys were for girls only or boys only. The first teddy bear saw the light of day in Germany. It was made by a seamstress named Margarete Steiff.

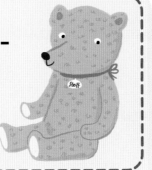

7 Snow and Rain

The popular game Fire, Water, Storm, Lightning can be changed in various ways, of course. We might add rain, snow, and or a scorching sun. Players let their imaginations run wild.

6 Fire, Water, Storm, Lightning

Flashes of lightning! Help! Make yourself as small as you can. When the water comes, you must climb to avoid it—maybe by climbing on the table. Now there's a fire; protect yourself by lying on the floor. If it's windy, hold on to something firm. One of the players summons fire, water, storm, or lightning, and the others do as he or she tells them. The slowest becomes the summoner in the next round.

5 Cat and Mouse

The jolly game of Cat and Mouse is especially popular with younger kids. All players but the Cat and the Mouse stand together in a circle. The Cat runs about outside the circle, while the Mouse may enter it if the circle allows. The aim of the game is for the cat to catch the mouse as quickly as possible.

4 Sardinen

I'm running to find a hiding place while the others count to 30. Their task is to find me. When one of them does, they will join me in my hiding place. This place will become ever more cramped as we are found by more and more seekers. The game ends with all players packed together like sardines in a can, which is why it is called Sardines.

Israeli Games

HI! MY NAME'S **HANNAH**, AND MY HOME IS IN **ISRAEL**. HERE, WE HAVE A LOT OF JEWISH HOLIDAYS, AND DURING THESE HOLIDAYS WE PLAY A LOT. BEST OF ALL, PARENTS AND GRANDPARENTS JOIN OUR GAMES. QUITE SIMPLY, THE WHOLE FAMILY HAS FUN!

1 Three Sticks

This traditional game is pretty good exercise, whether played indoors or out. Three sticks are laid on the ground. The goal is to jump in the gaps between them, touching the ground only once. The sticks are spread further and further apart, so that by the end it is practically impossible to manage each gap with only one footfall. If you don't believe me, try it yourself.

2 The magic dreidel

Let me begin by explaining that a dreidel is a four-sided spinning top made of clay or wood. It has a letter of the Hebrew alphabet on each side. The first of these letters means "nothing," the second "all," the third "half," and the fourth "put in."

3 Playing with a dreidel

We play this traditional Israeli game during the Hanukkah holiday. Everyone gets a certain number of chocolate coins. Before the game, each player puts one coin into the central "pot." Then a player spins the dreidel and follows the instructions on the side facing up when it stops spinning. The player may end up taking all of the chocolate from the pot, putting in more, taking half, or taking nothing.

4 Hanukkah

Hanukkah is an eight-day festival commemorating the miracle of the oil. It is said that the ancient Jews arrived at their temple to find only one pot of oil, enough to last one day. Owing to a miracle, however, the oil burned for eight whole days. For this reason, during Hanukkah we burn candles in our homes and prepare special dishes cooked in oil.

18

10 Think about your past

Dreidels are played with during Hanukkah not only for entertainment and the sweet rewards they bring, but also because they remind us of our past and traditions.

9 Charades

Every Shabbat we play the miming game Charades. The rules are simple: you think of a word (for an occupation, an activity, etc.) and try to act it out to the other players, without speaking. Although it sounds easy, presenting the given thing so that others understand your meaning can be really difficult!

8 Telephone

If you think that you have great hearing and a good memory, try playing Telephone, in which each player whispers to the next a phrase thought up by the first player. The phrase the last player speaks aloud will be really interesting! No matter what, the phrase always comes out all mangled.

7 Fill It Up

Can you pour water from one container into another using only a spoon held in your mouth? This fun game is bound to liven up your Shabbat afternoon!

5 Shabbat

Shabbat is another important holiday— Judaism's day of rest. It is our custom on the afternoon and evening of Shabbat to meet friends and play various games, thus spending the holiday in the best possible mood.

6 Elephant Bowling

One of these Shabbat games is Elephant Bowling, which sometimes makes me laugh so much my whole body hurts. We put bottles filled with water on the floor. Then we put a tennis ball in a long sock or stocking, which we put on our head. Now, when we move our head, the ball swings gently. We try to use the ball to knock over as many bottles as we can, without using our hands.

Indian Games

HI! MY NAME'S **SAMAY**, AND I LIVE IN **INDIA**. ALTHOUGH I ENJOY SCHOOL, MORE THAN ANYTHING I LOOK FORWARD TO THE AFTERNOON, WHEN I DASH OUTSIDE TO PLAY TRADITIONAL INDIAN GAMES. YOU'RE WELCOME TO JOIN ME IF YOU LIKE!

1 Marbles and Lakhoti

I never leave home without a handful of marbles in my pocket. My friends and I like no game more than Lakhoti, an ancient pastime for which marbles are essential. We prefer glass marbles to clay ones, which aren't so accurate.

2 How is Lakhoti played?

There are different forms of Lakhoti. Our favorite version is one where we draw a circle on the ground and set the marbles around it. Then we step up to a line, from where we shoot one marble in an attempt to hit as many of the marbles in the circle as possible, thereby knocking them out.

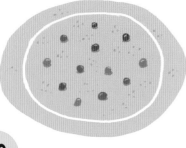

9 Poshampa

Poshampa, too, is great fun! Two players face each other, joining hands to make a gate-like structure. As they sing the Poshampa song, other players pass through the gate. As soon as the song ends, the first two players drop their arms, imprisoning the player passing through the gate and eliminating them from the game.

HELLO, I AM **SAMAY**

3 It's all about accuracy

Believe it or not, Lakhoti requires great concentration and patience as you focus on your goal. Your accuracy gradually gets better as you play. All this perhaps explains why this thousand-year-old Indian game has spread throughout the world and remains popular today.

8 Dancing dolls

The dancing Thanjavur doll is one of India's favorite toys. As it dances, it wobbles its head. It's great fun to watch it spin!

If you like jumping, draw a grid on the ground and toss a pebble into it. The player must jump to the place where the pebble has fallen without touching any of the grid's lines. Playing this game sometimes makes us sweat from the effort.

6 Stones

Girls excel at a game of five stones called Gutte. It begins when a player tosses one stone into the air, then gathers as many stones from the ground as she can before catching the tossed one. Next, along with the first stone, the player tosses the stones she has gathered, apparently making it impossible for her to gather the remaining stones. How girls can do this, I just don't know! The game requires quick reactions and agility.

4 Lattu

My friend Aarav is a true master at Lattu. To play the game, you wind a string around the tip of a colored, cone-shaped object (a top) and toss this groundward while holding the string so that the string unwinds as the top falls. If you do it right, the top will spin beautifully. The longer it spins, the better.

5 Traditional products

Aarav's grandfather has carved and decorated wooden kanchu tops his whole life. So it's hardly surprising that Aarav is our champion Lattu player!

21

Japanese Games

HI! MY NAME'S **AIKO**, AND I LIVE IN **JAPAN**—A LAND WITH THOUSANDS OF YEARS OF TRADITION AND BEAUTIFUL FLOWERING CHERRY TREES. I LIKE NOTHING MORE THAN TO PLAY AND HAVE FUN! WANT TO TAKE A LOOK AT TRADITIONAL JAPANESE GAMES AND TOYS? YOU DO? THEN COME WITH ME!

1 Origami

Like every Japanese child, I have loved to create various motifs and shapes in paper since my preschool days. I make animals, plants, and figures in many different sizes. Origami may look easy at first glance, but it requires a lot of thought and patience.

2 Long history

Origami, the technique of folding paper into decorative shapes, was first practiced as long ago as the 9th century CE, when it served as ornamentation in Shinto temples and religious ceremonies.

3 Kendama

The traditional game of Kendama requires the same patience and dexterity as Origami. The aim is to catch a wooden ball in a cup. The most skilled players manage to catch the ball on the pointed tip of the toy.

11 Double good fortune

To ensure good fortune, a thousand-plus years ago mothers would give their daughters beautiful balls made from old clothes, most notably silk kimonos—called temari balls—at New Year. In later times, these balls were ornamented with colorful embroidery; the making of temari balls became an art form in itself. My ball was given to my grandmother many years ago, when she was a little girl.

HELLO, I AM **AIKO**

4 Parts of the Kendama toy

A Kendama toy is made up of three parts—the tama (ball), the sarado (cup), and the ken (handle)—all held together by a string with a bead on the end. When you play Kendama for the first time, it will not go well. If you practice with patience, however, you may eventually become a Kendama master who performs wonders with this wooden toy.

10 Guaranteed good fortune

Hanetsuki was traditionally played by girls during the New Year's celebrations. It is said that the longer the player keeps the shuttle-cock (called the hane) in the air, the more protection she gains from evil demons and ill-fortune. Who knows? Maybe it's true . . .

9 Hanetsuki

The game of Hanetsuki also has a tradition of a thousand-plus years. It is played with a special paddle called a hagoita and a shuttlecock. The single player or two players aim to keep the shuttlecock in the air for as long as possible by striking it with the paddle.

8 Strings and shells

Japanese boys spin their tops by means of a string nearly two feet long, as do kids elsewhere in the world. In the 17th century, when this game was first played in Japan, the top was a spiral-shaped shell filled with sand. The shells were sealed with wax to prevent spillage.

7 Beigoma

Japanese boys have loved the spinning-top game Beigoma for centuries. The playing surface is a canvas sheet stretched over a large container. Players spin their top on this sheet. The winner is the player whose top spins the longest.

5 Otedama

What fun we girls have playing Otedama! It is played with five small bags filled with beans. We toss these to the ground. Then we throw one bag into the air. Before we catch it, we must pick up another bag from the ground. And so it goes until we have picked up all the bags.

6 A girls' tradition

Otedama came to Japan from China in the 8th century CE. Its rules were passed down from mother to daughter, and from grandmother to granddaughter. The game becomes ever more difficult with each round. By the end, it looks something like juggling.

23

Australian Games

GOOD DAY FROM **AUSTRALIA**. MY NAME'S **JARRAH**, AND I'M ABORIGINAL, MEANING MY FAMILY AND I ARE INDIGENOUS PEOPLE WHOSE ANCESTORS WERE THE FIRST INHABITANTS OF OUR COUNTRY. LET ME SHOW YOU SOME OF OUR TRADITIONAL GAMES.

1 Battendi

In this game, you throw a tennis ball with the goal of hitting a target as many times as possible. You use a pole with a cup on its end. It takes a steady hand, let me tell you.

2 Hunters of the future

In the past, Battendi provided Aboriginal children with important preparation for the hunt. They would throw a spear, not balls, at the target.

3 Mer Kai

The players form a circle and toss a ball into the air. Then they do all they can to keep the ball from hitting the ground. The ball pings off palms and various other body parts, depending on the player's skills.

10 Whagoo

Despite the odd name, it's actually a simple game of hide-and-seek. We aboriginal kids love this game, as do kids all over the world.

HELLO, I AM JARRAH

4 Kalq

In earlier times, players of this men's game would try to deflect their opponent's spear with their own. These days, however, the aim of the game is to volley the ball as many times as you can without it hitting the ground. You can play alone or in a circle of friends who pass the ball back and forth.

9 Yiri

Without lots of practice, you will always come last in this game. The aim is to throw a tennis ball into a rotating tire. If you were thinking that hunters used to practice accuracy by throwing their spears at a moving target, you would be right.

8 Kee'an

In this game, players in the past tried to throw a bone attached to some twine over a net and into a hole beyond, without the bone or the twine touching the net. These days, the bone and twine have been replaced by a ball attached to a ribbon—but that doesn't make things easier, believe me!

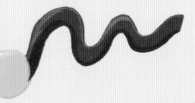

7 Tarnambai

In spring, Aboriginal children love collecting fluffy seeds of spinifex grass. They throw it into the air and then try to catch as much of it as they can.

5 Boomerang

These days, the boomerang is a fun toy. In the past, however, it was a dangerous hunting weapon.

6 Bubberah

For this game, a boomerang is essential. You wait your turn before throwing your boomerang and then standing motionless, waiting for it to come back. The winner is the thrower whose boomerang lands closest to them.

Games of Native Americans

HI! MY NAME'S **KOKO**, AND I'M A MEMBER OF THE INDIGENOUS NAVAJO TRIBE OF **AMERICA**. I'M PROUD TO CARRY ON OUR TRADITIONS. DO YOU KNOW ANYTHING ABOUT THE GAMES PLAYED BY ME AND MY ANCESTORS—KIDS AND GROWN-UPS ALIKE? NO? THEN LET ME TELL YOU ABOUT SOME OF THEM. COME ALONG!

1 God's favor

Long ago, the indigenous tribes of North America played games to please the gods: summoning rain, providing for a good harvest, driving away evil spirits, etc. Men played with men and women played with women, even though the games had the same rules for boys and girls.

2 Bear race

A bear race? This will be fun! You must step up to the starting line and wait for your cue. Your running style should look as much as possible like the gait of a bear. When you step forward with your right leg, your left arm should follow suit, and vice versa. The winner is not only the fastest but also the most bear-like.

HELLO, I AM
Koko

3 Bullroarers

Indigenous North American tribes (kids and grown-ups alike) played this game to summon rain. They held a cord attached to a slat that was almost five feet long. When this slat was swung rapidly over the head, the whistling sound it made was like a bull's roar.

4 Butterfly hide-and-seek

To play this game, you need some sticks and two stones. One of the stones is marked. One player holds out their closed hands, each of which contains one of the stones. The other player must guess which hand is holding the marked stone. If they guess wrong, they receive a penalty stick.

10 Luck or skill?

The games of North American tribes could be divided into two groups: games of chance (decided by a throw of the dice, for instance) and games of skill. Even so, our less gifted players had no cause for despair: the purpose of all these games was gradual self-improvement.

9 Toe Toss Stick

This simple game was popular with the Apache tribe. The aim was to toss a wooden stick vertically, as high as possible, but with such accuracy that it fell to earth at a specific point. Before the toss, the stick was balanced carefully on the player's big toe.

8 Frog races

Since nature has always been the great teacher for our tribes, we have historically held frog races. Racers assumed a position with their fingers around their ankles before hopping toward the finish line without falling or releasing their grip on their ankles.

7 Quiet as a butterfly

Wow, a butterfly! Since it was traditionally considered good luck for a butterfly to land on you, the girls of ancient tribes tried to be quiet and calm in the hope of attracting such a visit to their shoulders. The first girl so honored was declared the winner.

6 Moccasin game

You can also have a lot of fun with four soft leather shoes—called moccasins—and a single stone. The players draw lots to decide who will hide the stone in one of the moccasins. When hiding the stone, this player tries to confuse the others about where it is. The game is accompanied by the singer, a player chosen to encourage teammates and mock opponents in loud song.

5 Laughing game

The aim of this traditional game is to make your opponent laugh as quickly as possible. You do this by sitting opposite them and pulling all kinds of faces. The player who bursts out laughing first is the loser.

South American Games

HI! MY NAME'S **MANUEL**. WELCOME TO **SOUTH AMERICA**. AS MY FAMILY MOVES ABOUT A LOT, I HAVE SPENT TIME ALL OVER THE CONTINENT. WHEREVER I GO, I HAVE FRIENDS WITH WHOM I PLAY THE TRADITIONAL GAMES OF THEIR COUNTRY. WHY NOT JOIN US?

10 Greasy Pole

The aim is to retrieve the flag from the top of a pole greased with fat. The climb is far from easy. But it's a little easier if you laugh the whole time.

1 Sapo

The traditional game of Sapo may be simple, but it's a lot of fun. You stand or sit at a table or box topped with many holes and the seated figure of a toad. You throw coins at the holes. If you succeed in throwing a coin into the open mouth of the toad, you are the clear winner.

HELLO, I AM MANUEL

2 Magic toad

Members of the Incan culture, which once thrived in South America, believed that the toad had magical powers. Whoever presented a toad with a coin would have a wish fulfilled by that toad. Maybe this legend lies behind the popular game of Sapo.

3 Queimada

The great Brazilian game of Queimada is a lot like dodgeball. The playing area is divided into two halves, each end of which is a "cemetery." From their team's cemetery, a player throws a ball toward their opponents, who try to catch it and throw it back. If an opponent is struck by the ball rather than catching it, they are "killed" and must spend the rest of the game in the cemetery.

9 Onion

The more players who take part in this Ecuadorean game, the better. The kids sit on the ground. The first in line holds a stick or a tree; the second holds on to the first, and so on. The last player tries to break the chain by pulling the kids apart. When they succeed, it looks like an onion being peeled.

8 Burrito San Andrés

This game is especially popular in Ecuador. One of the players stands with their back to the wall, representing the head of a donkey. Six other players twist their bodies to form the donkey's body. The remaining players try to jump onto the donkey's back. The greater the number of players who succeed, the greater the fun—as I know very well!

7 Atrapar la cola

This traditional Chilean game is played by two teams of kids. Each team forms a "snake" as each player grabs the hips of a teammate. The last player in each line has a scarf attached to their waist to represent the snake's tail. On command, the snakes begin to chase each other, the aim being to get to the opponent's tail and seize the scarf. Neither snake may separate, nor may its parts change their positions.

6 Origins in the Andes

Chaza has a long history—it is 500 years old. It was a popular game with many indigenous inhabitants of South America.

5 Chaza

Have you ever seen such a big racket? Not only is it large, but it is also really heavy. Known as a bombo, it is used in Ecuador and Colombia to play the game of Chaza, which is like volleyball and tennis.

4 Balloon game

Having tied balloons around their ankles, players rush at each other and try to burst the balloons of their opponents. This fun game is very popular in Chile.

Scottish Games

HI! MY NAME'S **OLIVIA**. GREETINGS FROM THE **SCOTTISH HIGHLANDS**. AS IT'S A FINE DAY, I'M PLAYING OUTDOORS WITH MY FRIENDS. WE'D LIKE TO SHOW YOU SOME GAMES OUR MUMS AND DADS PLAYED, AND HOW WE PLAY THEIR GAMES TODAY. SO, WHAT ARE YOU WAITING FOR?

10 What Is It?

Your friends blindfold you before putting various objects in your hands and asking you to guess what they are. Your senses of smell, touch, and taste will help you with this.

HELLO, I AM **OLIVIA**

1 Bools: Good old marbles

Marbles have been popular with boys and girls since time immemorial. We Scots call them bools. In our version of the game, one player throws their bool and then a second tries to hit it, or at least get close to it, with their own throw. After a successful hit, the shooter takes possession of the opponent's marble. The one who ends up with the most bools is the winner.

2 Plainy Clappy

We girls play a lot of Plainy Clappy. All you need for it is an ordinary wall and a small ball. In the first round, we throw the ball against the wall and catch it when it comes back. In the second round, we clap before we catch the ball. In the third, we turn around while the ball is in the air. And so it goes, with our tasks becoming ever more difficult.

3 British Bulldog

This game is pretty exciting. One player is chosen to stand in front of the rest. The game begins when this player shouts, "British bulldog. One, two, three!" The other players then make a run for the other end of the playing area, chased by the bulldog. Players caught by the bulldog become his helpers.

4 Red Rover

This game requires strength and strong alliances. Two teams line up against each other, their members holding hands. One team invites a member of the other to break their chain and run through. If the attempt fails, that player is taken prisoner.

9 Tig

Playing Tig is great exercise. One player (the chaser) tries to touch the others as they try to escape him. Not only do Tig players laugh a lot, but they sweat a lot too.

8 Hide-and-seek

Hide-and-seek games are popular all over the world. Scottish hide-and-seek has one seeker only. All the other players hide in the hope that the seeker will find them last.

7 Magic with string

Is sitting in a fort boring? No way! In our fort, we tell each other scary stories, or we make string figures between our outstretched fingers. This game, called Cat's Cradle, is enjoyed by both girls and boys.

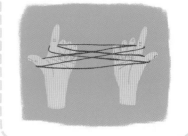

6 Building a fort

All kids enjoy building forts and hiding places, regardless of their age. They use whatever nature has provided, not least branches, sticks, and stones. And what pride they take in their work! Hanging out in a hut you have made yourself is a big adventure.

5 What's the Time, Mr. Wolf?

This is a classic Scottish game. The child playing the Wolf begins alone at the far end of the area, with his back to the others. When they ask for the time, the Wolf replies with a number. The others approach the Wolf by taking the same number of steps. The Wolf then cries, "Dinner-time!" then turns to face the other players and tries to catch those closest to him.

Dutch Games

HI! WELCOME TO THE **NETHERLANDS**, A LAND OF GREAT CHEESES, MAGNIFICENT TULIPS, ROMANTIC WINDMILLS, AND CLACKING CLOGS. OH SORRY, I FORGOT TO INTRODUCE MYSELF . . . MY NAME'S **LUCAS**. I'M GOING TO GO PLAY. WANT TO JOIN ME?

1 Koekhappen

Let's limber up with an old Dutch game. See that line with slices of ontbijtkoek (a traditional cake) hanging from it? It's at eye level, isn't it? Try eating a slice of cake without using your hands. The winner is the first to finish their slice.

2 Ontbijtkoek

Ontbijtkoek, the cake used in the game of Koekhappen, is a traditional Flemish and Dutch cake spiced with cloves, ginger, and cinnamon. It is mostly served at breakfast, topped with butter like a slice of bread. It is also a very popular snack.

3 Appelhapen

Sometimes apples coated with syrup hang from the Koekhappen line instead of the gingerbread line, posing an even greater challenge to the eater.

10 The King's Games

We Dutch are very keen on play—and since 2013 we have had our King's Games to prove it! This day of competition begins with a healthy breakfast before the sports and traditional games commence.

HELLO, I AM **LUCAS**

4 Eierlopen

This traditional Dutch race requires a steady hand, patience, and precision. Competitors carry a raw egg on a spoon along a marked route before depositing it in a bucket. The winner is the one who completes this task the fastest. The egg must remain intact for the whole race, so the players must concentrate very hard.

9 Spijkerpoepen

The biggest fun of all is a game where we tie a string around our waist. Hanging from the back is a nail—making us look like we have a tail! Our task is to squat and feed the nail into a bottle, which is very difficult when you are laughing like crazy.

As well as being a popular pastime in the Netherlands, Sjoelbak is played in France, Belgium, Germany, and even the Czech Republic.

7 Sjoelbak

The aim of Sjoelbak is to shuffle a wooden board so that wooden disks (pucks) slide through open arches into boxes, thereby scoring points. The way in which these points are counted varies from family to family or group to group.

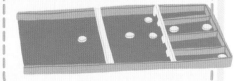

6 Blikgooien

This Dutch game, also a very old one, is all about being a good shot. You begin by building a tower out of tin cans. Then you throw a small ball at the tower, trying to knock over as many cans as possible on your first attempt. So simple, but great fun all the same!

5 Zaklopen

This sack race is my very favorite. The rules are not complicated. Each competitor climbs into a sack made of burlap or plastic before jumping in it to the finish line. It's important not to stumble or fall—if you do, you have to go back to the start.

Vietnamese Games

HI, AND WELCOME TO **VIETNAM**! MY NAME'S **DIEP**. I'D LIKE TO SHOW YOU OUR BEST-KNOWN KID'S GAMES. MAYBE YOU'LL LEARN THAT THEY ARE SIMILAR TO SOME OF YOURS. AS THE CASE MAY BE, YOU ARE SURE TO FIND THEM FUN!

1 The game of Dragon Snake

In this game, I'll play a doctor. A group of kids standing in a line, each holding the kid in front by the waist, will play a dragon. I, the doctor, must try to catch the kid who represents the Dragon Snake's tail. The others will try to prevent me from doing this.

2 The importance of cooperation

It's far from easy to catch the Dragon's tail, because all the children follow the movements of the first in an attempt to connect the head with the tail, thus forming a circle.

3 Nu Na Nu Nong

For this simple game, we all sing—and I love singing! We sit in a row with our legs stretched out in front of us. A fellow player (the leader) stands in front of us. As we sing our song, she pats our legs and feet. At the moment the song ends, the player she patted last must tuck in the leg in question. We play on until all legs are tucked in.

10 Nhay Day

My friends and I love jumping over a length of rubber stretched between two children (the "posts"). The aim of the game is to jump over this line from both sides, as high as possible. When the game begins, the rubber line extends between the ankles of one of the posts to the ankles of the other. The best of us can jump over a line at waist level.

HELLO, I AM **DIEP**

4 Nem Con

The throwing of a ball through a ring hanging from a tall bamboo tree is a ritual said to drive away sadness and suffering and to bring happiness. Don't worry if you don't manage to throw the ball through the ring at the first attempt—you can have as many tries as you want!

9 Dragons

Kites have been flown in Asia for thousands of years. Our ancestors believed that dragons, which kites represent, gave protection against evil and ill-fortune. For this reason, the names of diseases were written on kites' wings. It was believed that when the kite was released to the heavens, the dangers posed by these diseases were carried far away.

8 Kite parade

Children's kites tend to be quite simple paper ones. Adult kites are much more intricate. Many are not only covered with fabric but also fitted with windpipes of various sizes, which when in flight make a pleasing sound. You can sometimes imagine that a kite is singing!

7 Flying kites

We Vietnamese—kids and grown-ups alike—love flying kites, and we do so all year round, although it is best in summertime. One of us holds the string attached to the paper kite while a second runs with it against the wind . . . and moments later, the kite is soaring into the air.

6 Balls, not fruit

When we play Nem Con today, we throw special balls we make at home from fabric stuffed with rice and cotton seeds. To make balls heavier, we tie colorful tassels to them.

5 Legendary happiness

The Nem Con game emerged from a legend about Pia, a poor, troubled orphan. The story goes that Pia once went to the forest, where in his deep sorrow he threw a piece of fruit so hard and high that a fairy caught it in heaven. The fairy fell in love with Pia, before marrying him and bringing him happiness.

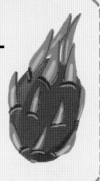

35

How Kids Play Around the World

Author: Štěpánka Sekaninová
Illustrator: Michaela Bergmannová
Translator: Andrew Oakland
Editor: Scott Alexander Jones

© B4U Publishing for Albatros,
an imprint of Albatros Media Group, 2023.
5. května 1746/22, Prague 4, Czech Republic
Printed in China by Leo Paper Group.
ISBN: 978-80-00-06795-7

www.albatrosbooks.com